The FIRST BOOK of

Other FIRST BOOKS you will enjoy

The FIRST BOOK of

WEEDS

by BARBARA L. BECK

Pictures by Page Cary

FRANKLIN WATTS, INC.
575 Lexington Avenue • New York 22

Library of Congress Catalog Card Number: 63-7584
© Copyright 1963 by Franklin Watts, Inc.
Printed in the United States of America
by Polygraphic Company of America

CONTENTS

WEEDS — FRIEND OR FOE?

WEEDS ARE plants of neglected land and waste places; or they are plants that live and thrive where we do not want them. They crowd out, damage, or destroy the plants we would prefer to grow. But if, by magic, every weed suddenly disappeared from the face of the earth, we would lose many truly beautiful and useful plants.

Imagine a countryside without the electric-blue flowers of chicory, the delicate pink-and-white flower cups of the wild morning glory (bindweed), and the dazzling golden heads of buttercups.

Many weeds have lovely flower colors and many more have dainty, intricate features such as the feathery heads of Queen Anne's lace, the graceful fronds of brake fern, or the tiny, furry leaves of mouse-ear chickweed.

We must remember that the plants that are called weeds in one locality are not necessarily considered weeds in another. In California, for instance, lupine is thought of as a weed; in parts of New England it is a favorite garden flower. Bluebonnets are weeds in Texas, but not in other states. This situation is true throughout the world, for climate and soil conditions have a great deal to do with whether or not a plant is called a weed.

In botany, the general study of plants, there is no classification or family of weeds, for they belong to a number of families containing many plants that are important to us. The Spurge Family, for example, besides the weed known as spotted spurge, includes many useful plants, some of which supply us with rubber and castor oil.

The usefulness of weeds cannot be denied. Many years ago, nearly every country home in Europe and Asia had an herb garden. Some of the plants mentioned in this book are herbs and were found in these gardens. Others were left to grow by the kitchen door. Dandelion, lamb's-quarters, and purslane, or pursley, were eaten much as we eat spinach or lettuce today. Many country people still gather them, and dandelion greens can be bought in many city markets. Some plants were used to flavor food; among them were peppermint, the mustards, and horehound, which still is used in making candy and cough drops.

Other plants in the herb garden were used in medicines. Long before the corner drugstore came into being, plants such as catnip, coltsfoot, yarrow, and wormwood were used in home remedies. People depended on the extracts from these and other plants to cure them of their illnesses. Today, foxglove supplies us with the heart drug called digitalis. A good many other plants are still used in medicines.

Weeds also act as soil binders. Their roots hold the soil and keep it from washing away in heavy rains or from blowing away in high winds. And weeds, when plowed under, are a kind of green manure, for they give back to the soil many of the minerals that the farmer needs to grow his crops. Perhaps it is well to remember here that only green plants, including countless numbers of weeds, are capable of storing the sun's energy. Without these green plants, human beings and animals could not live.

In spite of the weeds' often being beautiful, edible, and useful in preventing erosion, many people — sometimes understandably — think of them as harmful and something to be rid of. Truck farmers, for example, see no beauty in the yellow heads of mustard scattered

2

through acres of lettuce.

Many weeds are armed with extraordinary powers which do not add to their popularity. Some can make new plants by sending out underground runners. Others have drooping stems which root themselves wherever they touch the ground — we call this process "layering." Still others can even reproduce themselves from a piece of root. Many weeds can quickly replace lost parts; leaves whisked off by a lawn mower are speedily replaced by new ones.

Some weeds protect themselves by an unpleasant taste or odor, by sticky hairs, by thorns, and by chemicals that animals seem instinctively to know will hurt them or make them sick. Humans, too, find that the strong juices or chemicals in the roots, stems, leaves, flowers, or fruits of many weeds will poison them or irritate their skin.

A number of weeds act as hosts for insects and diseases that attack valuable crops. One such villain is the nightshade, which harbors the potato stalk borer as well as the disease known as potato mosaic. Both are ruinous to potato crops.

In short, weeds mean many things to many people . . . and like people they have both good and bad traits.

WHERE DO WEEDS COME FROM?

MANY, many millions of years ago, the first plants appeared on the face of the earth. By studying fossils we have learned that they did not look much like the plants we see today. Nonetheless, they were the ancestors of our present-day plants. Over an incredibly long period, they changed as there were changes in their environment. A kind of sorting-out process took place. Scientists call this "natural selection." The plants that were best suited to their environment were the ones that lived. Others, which could not adapt, for example, to a cooler climate or a dried-out soil, died. Modern weeds, as we know, are remarkable at adjusting to various soils and climates. But our environment changes very slowly — so slowly that usually we hardly know the change is happening. Still natural selection goes on; and who can tell whether, in thousands of years, the plants we know today will even exist on our earth.

HOW DO WEEDS GROW?

THE PLANTS mentioned in this book are made up of parts — roots, stems, leaves, flowers, and seeds. All of these parts have a job to do, and green plants as a whole do one of the most important jobs in all nature: they carry on photosynthesis. That is, they gather carbon dioxide from the air and take in water through their roots, and with the help of chlorophyll, a green substance in their leaves, they utilize the sun's energy to make simple sugars and starches. Plants use the sugars and starches as food for living, and store the surplus in their leaves and roots. Human beings and animals, in turn, eat plants as food from which they take energy.

Plant leaves come in assorted sizes and shapes. The drawings opposite show leaf shapes and arrangements. In order to identify a weed or any plant, a person should know the basic leaf shapes.

Oval-shaped

Lance-shaped

Tooth-edged

Narrow, oblong

Tooth-edged,
with parts deeply cut

Growing alternately
along a stalk

Round, with a
scalloped edge

Growing opposite
along a stalk

Each plant has its typical leaf shape. Leaves may grow opposite each other along the length of a stalk, or they may grow alternately on either side of a stalk.

Flowers are a little more complicated than leaves, as the drawings indicate. A typical flower grows on a receptacle, which is an enlarged part of the flower stalk. A flower usually — but not always — consists of four sets of flower parts: calyx, corolla, stamens, and pistils.

The *calyx,* or outside part, is generally made up of tiny green leaf-like *sepals,* which protect the flower bud. The calyx holds the *corolla,* usually a group of brightly colored *petals.*

Within the corolla are the male reproductive organs, called the *stamens,* which are often on long stalks called *filaments.* At the ends of the filaments are larger, boxlike parts called *anthers.* The anthers produce *pollen,* a fine yellow dust.

The female part of the flower is called the *pistil.* It consists of the *stigma,* the *style,* and the *ovary.* When pollen is caught on the surface of the stigma, it is carried down through the style (a tube) to the ovary, the enlarged base of the pistil, which contains undeveloped seeds called *ovules.* When the pollen joins the ovules, they are fertilized and seeds develop.

Flowers depend chiefly on insects to carry the pollen from the stamens to the pistils, although wind also helps. To attract insects, flowers have many devices, among them their colored petals. Many flowers also manufacture a sweet juice called *nectar,* which insects like as food. The nectar in flowers is placed so that an insect, to reach it, must brush by the stamens with their pollen. Unwittingly the insect collects pollen on its body and, in gathering more nectar, rubs the pollen off on the pistils of other blossoms. In this way, seedmaking becomes possible, and plants can reproduce their kind.

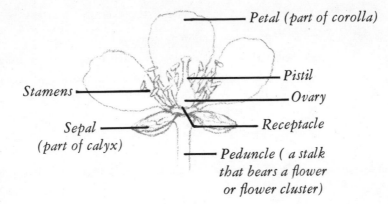

Petal (part of corolla)

Pistil

Stamens

Ovary

Sepal
(part of calyx)

Receptacle

Peduncle (a stalk
that bears a flower
or flower cluster)

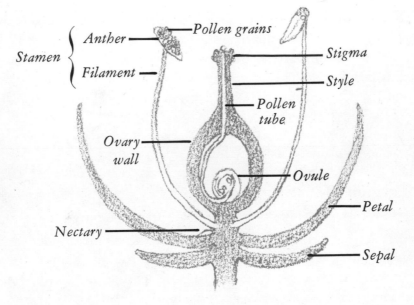

Stamen {

Anther

Pollen grains

Stigma

Filament

Style

Pollen
tube

Ovary
wall

Ovule

Petal

Nectary

Sepal

WEEDS IN THE LAWN

Chickweed
(Stellaria media)

A member of the Pink Family, this creeping annual may flower every month of the year. Some people call it winterweed, for it lives through mild northern winters. The tiny (¼-inch) white flowers appear only when the sun is shining, and each has 5 petals so deeply cleft that they seem to be 10. The 5 sepals are longer than the petals. Chickweed's many slender stems root themselves at the joints and form a thick tangle. If a person has the patience to pick the tiny leaves, he may boil and eat them.

Crabgrass
(Digitaria ischaemum, Digitaria sanguinalis)

Like the villain in a TV Western, crabgrass is despised by all and loved by none. Many grassy weeds are mistakenly called crabgrass by those who do not really know what this notorious weed looks like. There are two kinds to watch for: small crabgrass *(Digitaria ischaemum)* and large crabgrass *(Digitaria sanguinalis)*. They look very much alike, but small crabgrass is smooth and tends to be purplish, while large crabgrass is hairy. Watch for a long seedstalk with spreading, fingerlike spikes at the top. Both kinds of crabgrass turn reddish-brown in late summer. They are annuals, and one plant can produce as many as 50,000 seeds.

Creeping Buttercup, Sitfast
(Ranunculus repens)

Belonging to the Crowfoot Family, this fast-spreading weed is as stealthy as an Indian. It creeps up on a lawn, and before you know it the grass has lost out. At each joint the low, hairy stems root themselves to make new plants. The 5- to 9-petaled flowers are a brilliant, glossy yellow, with the varnished look typical of all the buttercups. The green leaves are 3-parted

*Chickweed
(creeping,
to 2½ feet long)*

*Crabgrass
(to 16 inches high)*

*Creeping buttercup
(creeping,
to 2 feet long)*

9

and may remind you of the footprint of a bird. This weed is also called creeping crowfoot.

Creeping Thyme
(Thymus serpyllum)

Considered a weed by some and a substitute for grass by others, this tiny plant makes a thick-napped, dark-green carpet no more than 1 inch high. Creeping thyme is most common in New England. The tiny, soft leaves are aromatic when stepped on. The dainty, fragrant, purplish flowers grow in whorls on upright spikes, and bloom from June to September. This plant is a first cousin to the herb, thyme, which is found on many kitchen shelves.

Curly Dock, or Yellow Dock
(Rumex crispus)

The pesky curly dock may grow as high as 3 feet if it isn't mowed, and it puts down a taproot 2 feet deep. This weed is easy to recognize because the edges of its blue-green leaves are wavy and curly. The long, loose leaves at its base are edible when gathered young and boiled. The roots, when dried and pulverized, may be used for cleaning the teeth. The small flowers, in clusters at the tops of the stems, are yellowish at first, then reddish-brown as October approaches. The little heart-shaped seeds are reddish-brown, too.

Dandelion
(Taraxacum officinale)

Who doesn't know the dandelion! Those bright-yellow heads and raggedy leaves are familiar to everyone. This hobo has an efficient way of reseeding itself. By the time blossoming is over, each part of the flower has been replaced by a white tuft of silky hairs, resembling an inside-out umbrella with a fat handle. To each tuft a seed is attached. With every puff of the wind, the downy hairs blow away, carrying the seeds far and wide. Dandelions are often called blowballs. Their more common name comes from the French

*Creeping thyme
(creeping,
to 8 inches long)*

*Curly dock
(to 3 feet high)*

*Dandelion
(flower spike,
to 6 inches high)*

dent de lion, or lion's tooth, so called because of the plant's sharply indented leaves. The young green leaves are good to eat in a salad, or boiled like spinach.

English Daisy, or Lawn Daisy
(Bellis perennis)

Often cultivated in the garden, English daisies grow and spread so fast that they are poor company for more well-behaved flowers and soon take over the whole garden. The lawn mower does not touch their low, spoon-shaped, downy leaves. The flowers rise from 3- to 8-inch stems, surrounded at the base by a circle of leaves called a rosette. The dainty little pink-and-white flowers bloom in the spring. English daisies frequently live through the winter in the North.

Ground Ivy
(Glechoma hederacea)

Also known as gill-over-the-ground or run-away-robin, this little trailing plant quickly spreads and takes command of a lawn. Three inches is about as tall as you'll ever see ground ivy. It makes a cool, green carpet under heavy shade trees and will stay green into December. This weed is not often seen in southern states. The flower clusters are purplish-blue, about 1 inch long, and blossom in spring and summer. The leaves are round or kidney-shaped, and scalloped. The plant is a close relative of catnip. Some botanists call it *Nepeta hederacea.*

Heal-all, or Self-heal
(Prunella vulgaris)

As its names suggest, this plant was thought by the ancients to have curative powers. During the Middle Ages and even later it was used to heal wounds and to cure many ailments, especially sore throats. Heal-all makes a lovely, semievergreen carpet, but it is a nuisance in the lawn. Flowering in July and August, the blossoms are violet or blue, or sometimes pinkish. The plant roots itself at the stem joints. Heal-all is a member of the Mint Family.

Ground ivy
(creeping,
to 18 inches long)

English daisy
(flower spike,
to 8 inches high)

Heal-all
(to 2 feet high)

13

Knotweed, or Knotgrass
(Polygonum aviculare)

If the soil of the lawn becomes packed down by much walking, then watch out for knotweed. With a host of tough, wiry stems bearing lancelike leaves at their ends, knotweed will form a thick, blue-green mat. One plant may grow to a diameter of 4 feet. Its tiny flower parts are pale-green or whitish, with a trace of pink, and appear in slender clusters from June to October. Despite its name, knotgrass, this weed is not a grass but a member of the Buckwheat Family. An ancient superstition tells us that regular eating of knotweed seeds will stunt one's growth. The Latin name *aviculare* means "small birds," and refers to the small birds' habit of eating the seeds.

Mouse-ear Chickweed
(Cerastium vulgatum)

Cerastium comes from the Greek and means "little horn." This weed is probably so named because its seedpods look somewhat like tiny powder horns. It is a creeping plant and not a true chickweed of the genus *Stellaria*, as is the chickweed mentioned earlier. Its small, furry leaves are like a mouse's ears: hence the first part of its English name. The leaves grow opposite each other and are spoon-shaped. The pretty white flowers cluster at the tops of the stems from May to October.

Nut Grass, and Yellow Nut Grass
(Cyperus rotundus, and Cyperus esculentus)

Their deep rootstocks, slender runners, and underground tubers or nutlets, make these plants, members of the Sedge Family, tough opponents for any lawn. You can recognize nut grass by its umbrellalike flowering heads. The spikelets (flower groups) in nut grass are purplish-brown, while yellow nut grass has straw-colored flowers. The "nuts," or tubers, of yellow nut grass may be eaten, and taste a good deal like almonds. They are sometimes found

Knotweed
(to 2 feet long)

Mouse-ear chickweed
(creeping,
to 18 inches long)

Nut grass
(to 2 feet high)

for sale in Italian marketplaces. The seeds of both plants are often carried long distances by overflowing streams, to take root in new areas. This weed is closely related to the water-loving *Cyperus papyrus,* the plant used by the ancient Egyptians for making paper.

Common or Broad-leaved Plantain, and Narrow-leaved Plantain or Buckhorn
(Plantago major and Plantago lanceolata)

The plantains, according to ancient lore, were known as "devil's shoe-strings," and it was believed that whenever the plant appeared, the Devil was nearby. The American Indians called common plantain "Englishmen's weed" or "whiteman's foot," for wherever Englishmen settled, this weed was sure to be. The broad-leaved and the narrow-leaved plantains do not look like each other. The broad-leaved plantain has oval, strongly veined, often purplish leaves; the other plantain's leaves are ribbonlike and hairy, but also heavily veined. The flowers are different, too. Common plantain has a fuzzy stem with a long, thin flower spike. Narrow-leaved plantain has a bare stem topped by a shorter spike of flowers. Plantains make themselves very much at home in gardens.

Witchgrass, or Quack Grass
(Agropyron repens)

Try pulling up witchgrass, and you'll find that about 4 inches below the earth's surface this wiry monster has put down straw-colored rootstocks that spread several yards in every direction. If you leave even the smallest piece of root behind, it will grow a new plant. The seeds of this weed live a long time, too. They may be inactive for four years and then suddenly produce a new plant. Witchgrass leaves have smooth sheaths, and the blades are rough on the upper sides.

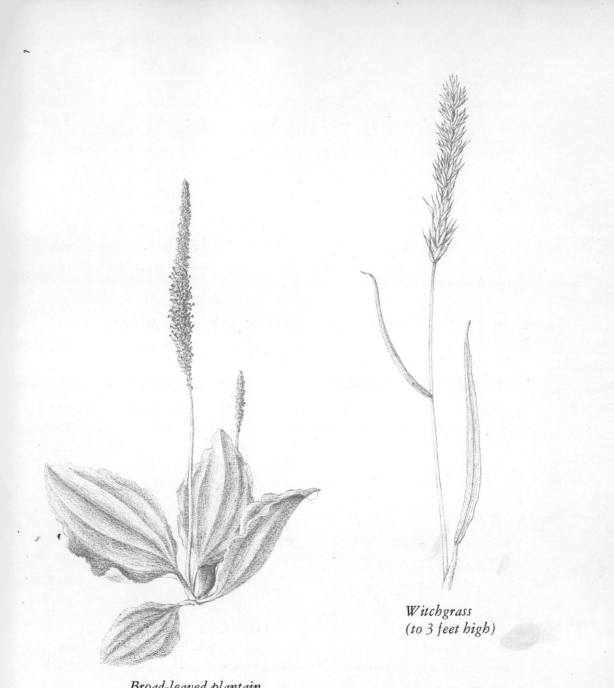

Witchgrass
(to 3 feet high)

Broad-leaved plantain
(flower spike,
to 10 inches high)

17

Spotted Spurge
(Euphorbia maculata or Euphorbia nutans)

The botanical name *Euphorbia* comes from Euphorbus, the famous Greek physician to King Juba, who fought for Pompey, the Roman general. Plants of the Spurge Family have a milky, somewhat acrid juice which may blister a person's skin. Spurges are beautiful to look at; many of them are poisonous, however. Animals will not eat spotted spurge. Its red spots, near the leaf stems, are thought to be shaped like the head of a fox. The leaves tend to be reddish and the small, white to reddish flowers are grouped in little clusters, appearing from July to September. Spurge is a relative of the lovely Christmastime plant, poinsettia.

FIELD, PASTURE, AND ROADSIDE WEEDS

Brake Fern, or Bracken
(Pteridium aquilinum)

Certainly one of the most widely distributed ferns in the world, the brake fern reproduces itself not by seeds, but by spores. The spores are small, primitive, one-celled reproductive bodies and are enclosed in a sac called a sporangium. There are many age-old beliefs about what can be seen in the rootstock of a brake fern cut horizontally. Try it the next time you come across this plant in a dry, sun-baked field. Brake fern foliage is poisonous to animals.

Butter-and-eggs, or Yellow Toadflax
(Linaria vulgaris)

This weed is also called wild snapdragon, for its flowers are shaped like those of the garden snapdragon. They are a cheerful sight in a meadow. Each 2-lipped blossom is yellow with an orange throat. The narrow leaves are blue-green and rather straggly. This plant blooms from June to October, and throughout the winter even though it looks shriveled up and dead it releases many flat, black seeds from its brown pods.

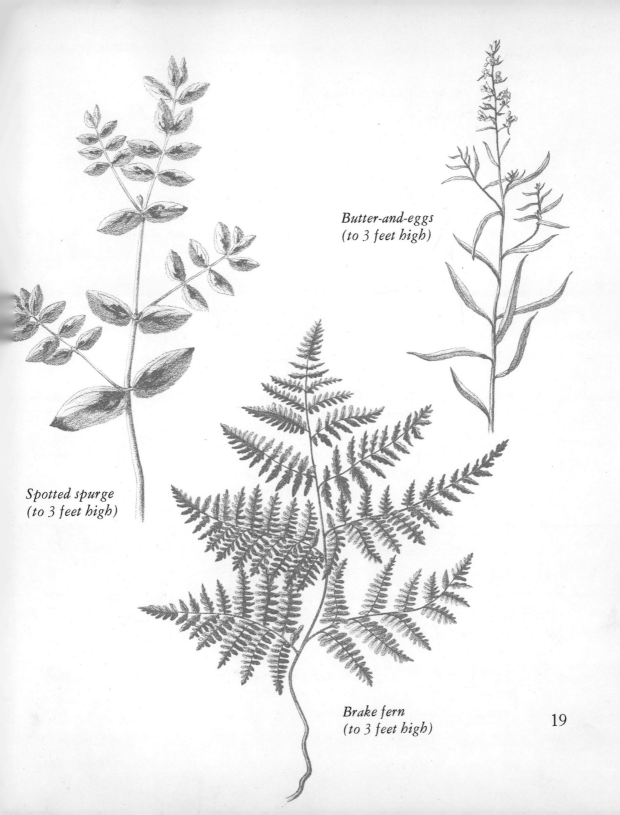

Butter-and-eggs
(to 3 feet high)

Spotted spurge
(to 3 feet high)

Brake fern
(to 3 feet high)

19

Tall, or Common, Buttercup
(Ranunculus acris)

In spring the glossy, golden heads of the buttercup appear like patches of sunshine in our fields and pastures. These weeds are so enchanting that we must forgive them their poisonous qualities. This buttercup has been given another name, blister plant, because it blisters the mouths of animals who may eat it. Most animals do not eat buttercups, however, and the plants go to seed, with the result that in time an entire pasture may appear carpeted with the dazzling weed.

Burdock
(Arctium lappa)

One of the biggest weeds of all, the burdock may stand 8 feet high. A single leaf measures 7 or 8 inches across and 12 to 18 inches long. Burdock is a biennial: that is, it lives for only two years. But its round burs — its seed receptacles — attach themselves to furry animals and are carried for miles to begin life anew. This weed's Latin name, *Arctium,* originally came from the Greek word for bear. Its second name, *lappa,* means bur. Possibly the name refers to the way the seeds are carried. *Lappa* is also the name given burdock roots, used in some blood medicines. Every country child has probably fashioned little baskets from the plant's sticky burs.

Cinquefoil
(Potentilla simplex)

A "once-upon-a-time" remedy for an aching tooth, cinquefoil roots have some narcotic qualities. Because the many-toothed leaves are made up of 5 fingerlike leaflets, silky on their undersides, cinquefoils are also called five-fingers. The calyxes are 5-cleft, with 5 bractlets (tiny leaflets), so that they appear to be 10-cleft. Each corolla has 5 separate yellow petals. Cinquefoil plants growing abundantly in a dry field or an old meadow usually indicate an acid soil.

20

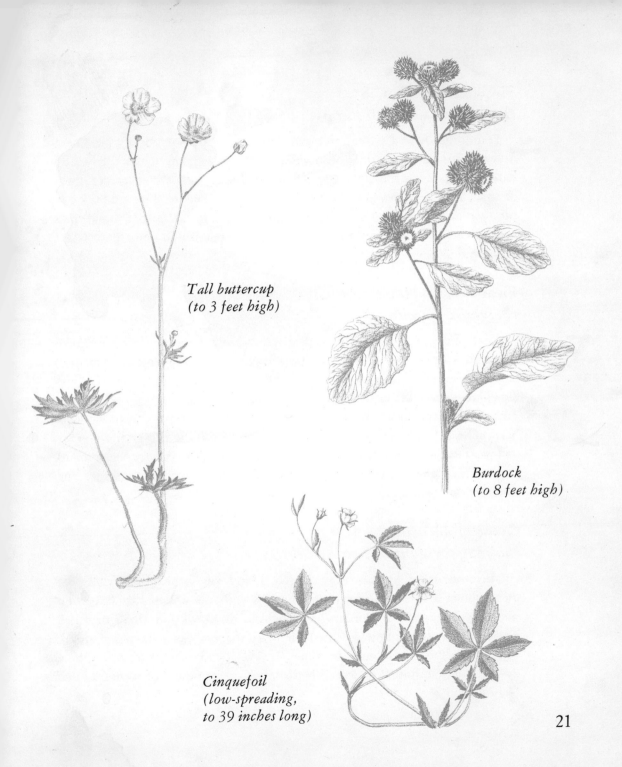

*Tall buttercup
(to 3 feet high)*

*Burdock
(to 8 feet high)*

*Cinquefoil
(low-spreading,
to 39 inches long)*

21

Fireweed
(Epilobium angustifolium)

Found mostly in Canada, northern America, and along the Pacific Coast, fireweed has another name, burntweed. Both names come from this weed's habit of appearing rapidly in clearings after forest fires or the cutting down of trees. It is a member of the Evening Primrose Family. Fireweed's pretty summer flowers have 4 purplish-magenta petals. In California, beekeepers raise fireweed as a honey plant. Its stems are reddish in color and rather tough and woody.

Fleabane, or Horseweed
(Erigeron canadensis)

Sometimes rising 6 feet high, fleabane is known the world over. There are many species of this weed. Its upper leaves are narrow and lance-shaped, its lower leaves wider and toothed. The flowers, which appear in May and June, are borne aloft in such a way as to suggest a horse's tail. There are over 100 small, greenish-white ray flowers, appearing at the margins of a flower head. The disk flowers — the ones in the center of the flower head — are yellow. Fleabane's leaves produce an oil that fleas do not like — hence its name. The plant also contains a chemical that may cause smarting eyes and skin rashes.

Giant Goldenrod
(Solidago gigantea)

There are many species of goldenrod. Hay fever victims well know the great, showy clusters of tiny yellow flowers with the pollen that brings on sneezing. They seem to appear everywhere in meadows and along roadsides in summer and autumn. Each of their lance-shaped leaves has three strong veins. By boiling the flowers in water, the American Indians made a yellow dye for their clothing. Goldenrod is the official state flower of Kentucky and Nebraska.

22

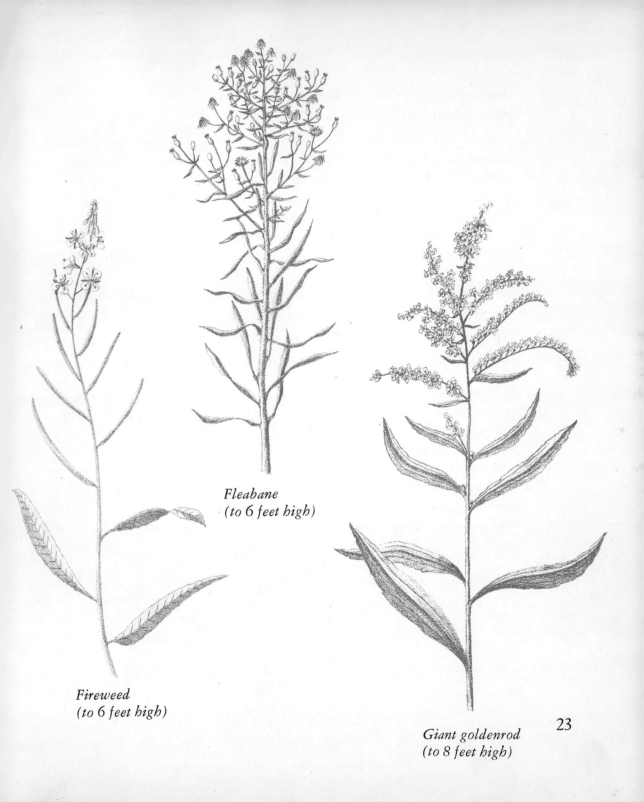

Fleabane
(to 6 feet high)

Fireweed
(to 6 feet high)

Giant goldenrod
(to 8 feet high)

23

Orange Hawkweed, or Devil's Paintbrush
(Hieracium aurantiacum)

When these familiar orange-red flowers go to seed, they produce a down that flies "every which way," and so the wind scatters seeds to all corners of the field. The stems are covered with rough hairs; the leaves — in a rosette at the base of the plant — bristle, too. The juice of the hawkweed is milky. As with all members of the large Composite Family, hawkweed's small flowers are grouped into heads, surrounded by small, scalelike leaves. Yellow hawkweed (Hieracium pratense) looks much like its orange relative, and is just as common in our fields. The plants of this genus were named by people of ancient times who thought that hawks used to eat the weeds to strengthen their eyesight.

Hay-scented Fern
(Dennstaedtia punctilobula)

This graceful plant thrives in dry, sun-drenched fields. Hay-scented ferns have leaves, or fronds, that produce a fragrant wax. Animals do not like it, and so the plant is spared by them and spreads freely. Ferns never have flowers, but reproduce by creeping roots and by spores. You may find the tiny spore cases on the back of each frond; if you shake the plant, the ripened spores will fall off. Place them in a paper bag to dry, and after one or two weeks you may plant them, using a pot of good, moist soil with some sand mixed in. Transplant the tiny ferns to other pots when they begin to grow too close together.

Mullein, or Flannel Plant
(Verbascum thapsus)

Tall and stately, the mullein stands from 4 to 7 feet high. Large, flannel-like leaves form a rosette on the ground. As they ladder up the stalk, the leaves grow smaller but no less fuzzy. High above, masses of golden flowers

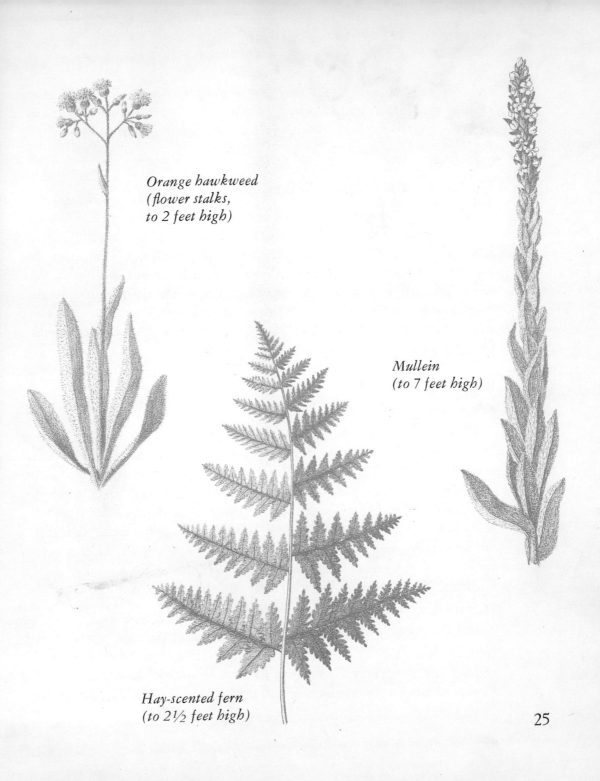

Orange hawkweed
*(flower stalks,
to 2 feet high)*

*Mullein
(to 7 feet high)*

Hay-scented fern
(to 2½ feet high)

25

on woolly spikes make this a truly beautiful weed. Another name for it is candlewick. Many years ago, peasants scraped the hairs from its leaves to use in making candlewicks. Mullein, when not in bloom, is often mistaken for foxglove *(Digitalis purpurea)*.

Queen Anne's Lace, or Wild Carrot
(Daucus carota)

Country people call this plant bird's nest because of the way the flower head curls at the edges after blooming. When the seeds ripen, the dry pods split upward, with each half containing a seed, which then flies off with the wind. The lovely, lacy flowers resemble a flat, white doily with a single purplish-black flower right in the center of each one. The leaves are like garden carrot leaves. Farm animals do not like this weed because it contains an acrid oil that tastes a good deal like turpentine.

Sagebrush
(Artemisia tridentata)

A native of our Great Plains and westward, sagebrush likes an arid climate. The rolling foothills, wide plains, and low mountains are its home. The woody, shrubby stems of sagebrush are covered with fine, silver-gray hairs. The plant, particularly its long silvery leaves, is aromatic when crushed. The flower heads are in crowded spikes which, when the seeds are ripe, fall and are blown for miles by the wind. To keep from dying during droughts, the sagebrush can shed all its leaves, thereby conserving its water supply.

Canada Thistle, and Bull Thistle
(Cirsium arvense, and Cirsium vulgare)

There is nothing meaner than a colony of Canada thistles. These weeds colonize themselves by means of creeping roots, and even the smallest piece of root will give rise to a new plant. As a result, they are hard to get rid of. Canada thistle's close relative, the bull thistle, has very prickly stems, while

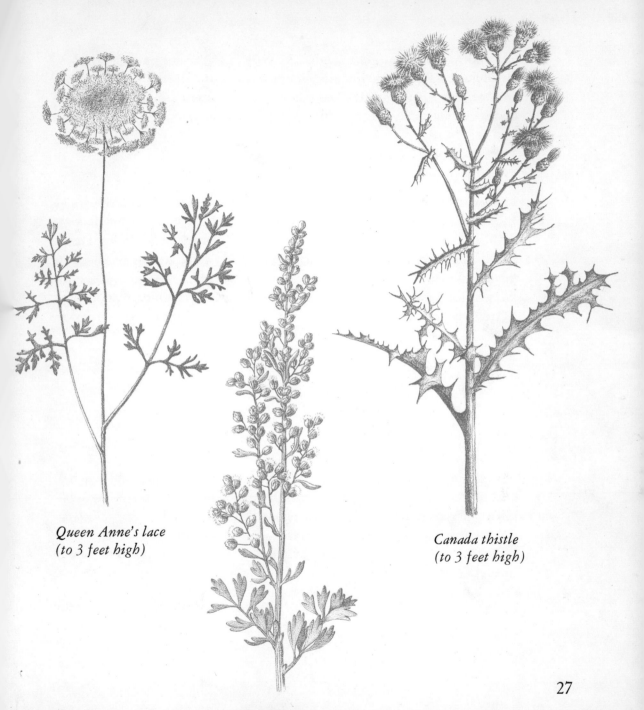

Queen Anne's lace
(to 3 feet high)

Canada thistle
(to 3 feet high)

Sagebrush
(to 10 feet high)

27

Canada thistle's stems are smooth. The bull thistle is not quite as mean in its growing habits as the other is. You will know the thistles by their spiny-toothed leaves and prickly flower heads. The flowers are usually pinkish-purple — sometimes white — and appear in late summer.

Yarrow, or Milfoil
(*Achillea millefolium*)

The leaves of yarrow are fernlike, and fragrant when crushed. When put on a wound, they are supposed to stop bleeding. According to mythology, Achilles applied leaves, probably yarrow, to the wounds of Telephus. Hence the plant's Latin name, *Achillea.* Later on, when Achilles was wounded in the heel by Paris, there apparently was no yarrow nearby. Another name for this plant is nosebleed, because of its reputed power of checking that ailment. Yarrow tea was used as a tonic by our ancestors. The flat-topped, lacy flower cluster is usually white, but sometimes pink.

WEEDS IN THE GARDEN

Bindweed
(*Convolvulus arvensis*)

Resembling the morning glory that wreathes our trellises and porches, field bindweed, as it is also called, is a troublesome plant with an incredibly large and strong root system. Aboveground, the honeyed, fragrant flowers and spear-shaped leaves please everyone, but belowground this fiend rules and robs the soil for many feet around. The lovely pink-and-white flower cups close when they are picked or when it rains, and also at nighttime. *Convolvulus* means "enwrap" in Latin. Just one of this plant's many twining stems can travel as far as 10 feet. It is sometimes called wild morning glory.

28

Yarrow
(to 2 feet high)

Bindweed
(climbing,
to 10 feet long)

29

Mayweed, or Dog Fennel
(Anthemis cotula)

Even before you see it, you may easily identify mayweed. Just step on it, and the trampled leaves give out an awful smell which may make you sneeze. The flower, appearing from June to October, is white with a yellow center. Animals who eat mayweed suffer blistered and burned mouths and noses, and some people who touch it break out with a rash similar to that caused by poison ivy. This weed belongs to the huge family called Composites, all of which have tiny blossoms arranged in such dense heads that they resemble a single flower.

Galinsoga, or Frenchweed
(Galinsoga ciliata)

A native of tropical America, galinsoga enthusiastically grows as far north as southern Canada. It is a lovely, graceful plant with white ray flowers and yellow disk flowers that appear in the late summer and fall. The leaves are opposite, rather oval-shaped, and toothed. Sometimes the upper leaves have no leafstalks. Galinsoga's stems may be straight and tall, to 2 feet; or they may droop onto the ground and root at the joints.

Common Mallow, or Cheeses
(Malva neglecta)

Have you ever tasted cheeses? When the petals fall from the 5-parted white flowers of the common mallow you will find the fruit or seeds arranged in a circle on a tiny, flat plate, as shown in the drawing on the opposite page. This looks like the round cheese that you might find in an old-fashioned country store. These seeds are edible while they are still soft. The plant hugs the ground and spreads to about 2 feet in diameter. The leaves, on long, slim stems, are gently lobed, with scalloped edges. Europeans and Mexicans eat them in salads. The mallow root is somewhat like ginseng, and may formerly have been used for medicinal purposes.

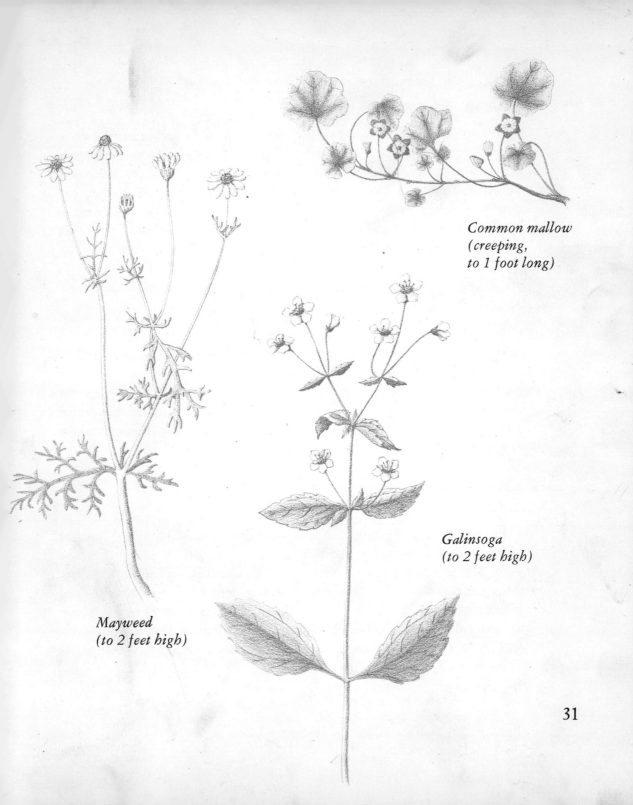

Common mallow
(creeping,
to 1 foot long)

Galinsoga
(to 2 feet high)

Mayweed
(to 2 feet high)

31

Pigweed
(*Amaranthus retroflexus*)

Not to be confused with lamb's-quarters, which is also called pigweed, this tall, bold weed trespasses everywhere. Pigs consider its leaves good eating, hence its name. The leaves are dull-green, with wavy edges, and are on long leafstalks. They droop and turn inward. In midsummer the small, green flowers, clustered on spikes, remind us of some members of the Grass Family. Pigweed seeds are a favorite food of winter birds. This weed is a first cousin to the western tumbleweeds.

Purslane, Pursley, or Pusley
(*Portulaca oleracea*)

Purslane has a little jewel box. When the seeds are ripe, the pod splits around the middle and the lid pops up, revealing dozens of wrinkled seeds, which the wind obligingly carries away. In summer, gardeners have their troubles with this thick-stemmed, fleshy-leaved weed. One plant may sprawl over the ground to a diameter of 10 inches. The pale-yellow flowers of purslane open only on sunny mornings, and only for a few hours. Purslane leaves are edible.

Groundsel, or Ragwort
(*Senecio vulgaris*)

Pliny, the ancient historian, claimed that a piece of groundsel root, cut off and placed on an aching tooth, would cure it. But there is a catch to the story. The remaining root must be replanted; if it dies, you are in for a trip to the dentist. The yellow flowers of this plant are followed by a white head of fluff, called a "pappus." Each bit of fluff is attached to a seed; this explains why, like dandelion seeds, those of groundsel are uncommonly good travelers. The Latin name, *Senecio,* comes from a word meaning "old man," and refers to the groundsel's white head of fluff.

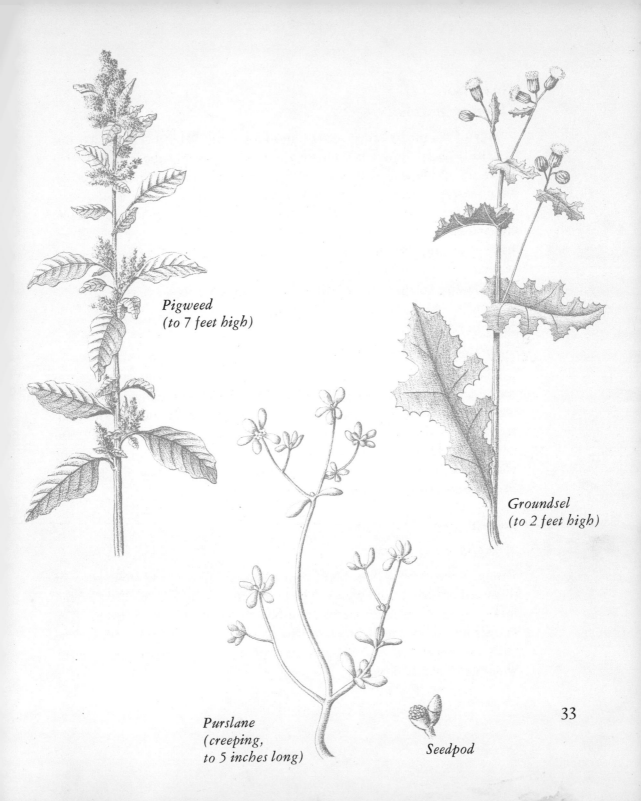

Pigweed
(to 7 feet high)

Groundsel
(to 2 feet high)

Purslane
(creeping,
to 5 inches long)

Seedpod

33

Sheep Sorrel
(Rumex acetosella)

Any of the plants called sorrels are sour-tasting. Why this particular one is called "sheep" sorrel is a mystery, although possibly the reason is that sheep and cattle are often poisoned by eating too much of it. This weed is single-sexed, or dioecious (dy-EE-shus), as botanists say. That is, the male plant, with more densely whorled, yellowish flowers, is entirely separate from the female plant, which has somewhat reddish flowers. The leaves are halberd-shaped; the lower part of each one is eared, as the fifteenth-century weapon called a halberd was. The leaves are used by some people in cream soups and in salads, but only when they are very young.

Shepherd's Purse
(Capsella bursa-pastoris)

This weed was named shepherd's purse because its seeds were thought to resemble the small leather pouches carried by shepherds many years ago. It is a funny-looking little plant with tiny, heart-shaped "purses" running up each single stalk after the flowers have faded and gone. Each "purse" contains a myriad of seeds. The young, dandelionlike leaves at the base of the plant are sometimes used in salads. The shepherd's purse plant appears early in the spring and is a true herald of the season.

Sow Thistle
(Sonchus oleraceus)

Rising perhaps to 10 feet high from a strong taproot, the stout stem of this weed contains a milky juice. The leaves are prickly and toothed and can make a nasty scratch. Europeans often boil the young leaves for eating. The flowers are somewhat like those of the dandelion, but are pale yellow. The seeds are topped by tattletale-gray tufts of fluff, which enable them to be wind-borne, and so to scatter.

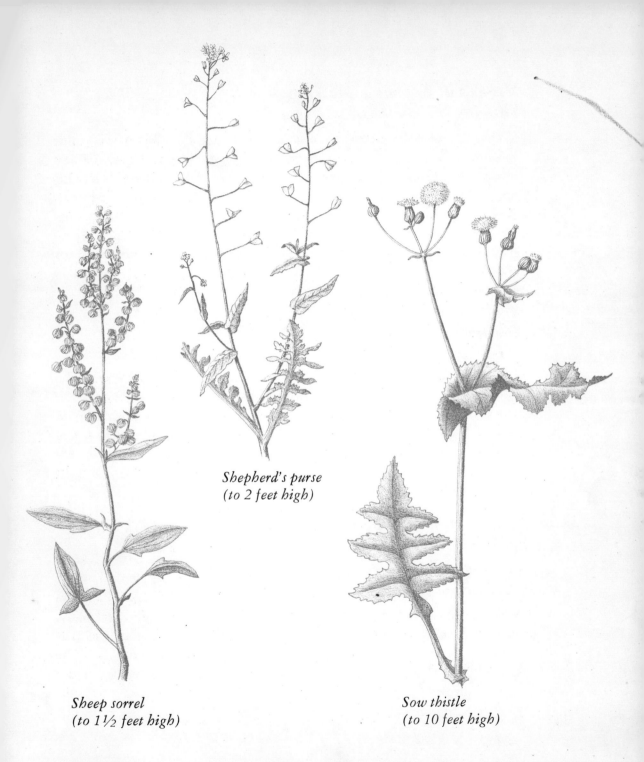

Shepherd's purse
(to 2 feet high)

Sheep sorrel
(to 1½ feet high)

Sow thistle
(to 10 feet high)

Velvetleaf, or Indian Mallow
(*Abutilon theophrasti*)

Here is a plant that loves our southern states and their warm, well-cultivated fields. This fast-growing giant, bearing great, heart-shaped, velvety leaves, will reach as high as 4 feet. The top of the seedpod resembles a block print and was used by our forefathers to make designs on rolls of butter. Because of this, velvetleaf is also known as butter print. It is also called pieprint and piemarker, because its pods were used to stamp the edge of piecrust. Velvetleaf seeds are known to have germinated after lying dormant for over fifty years.

Wild Lettuce, or Prickly Lettuce
(*Lactuca scariola*)

One feature of wild lettuce is the strange way its prickly leaves are turned up on edge. Known also as compass plant, this weed supposedly has some leaves that point south and some that point north. Unfortunately, without a compass it is hard to tell which leaves are which. The leaves and the stems are filled with a milky juice. When full-grown, wild lettuce may be 5 feet high. In the Bible, the "bitter herbs" used during the Passover were probably wild lettuce, chicory, dandelions, and sheep sorrel.

WEEDS YOU CAN EAT

Chicory
(*Cichorium intybus*)

Among chicory's many other names are blue sailors, succory, and bunk. Its dried roots are roasted and used as a coffee substitute and, years ago, merchants often cheated customers by putting inexpensive chicory into the ground coffee. Many Europeans, though, prefer chicory to coffee. The tender shoots may be blanched and used in salads. European farmers say this plant

Seedpod

Velvetleaf
(to 4 feet high)

Wild lettuce
(to 5 feet high)

Chicory
(to 4 feet high)

37

makes good hay for their livestock. You can't miss chicory's brilliant blue flowers, straggling along the stems. In some varieties, the flowers are pink or purplish.

Dandelion
(Taraxacum officinale)

Despite their nuisance value in the lawn, dandelions make fine eating. The young leaves may be boiled, and taste a little like spinach. Young dandelion greens are also good in salads. In Japan, these somewhat bitter leaves are occasionally substituted for mulberry leaves in feeding silkworms. The milky juice in the stem makes an excellent wine and, last but not least, the roots may be roasted, pounded down to a powder, and used as a substitute for coffee.

Horehound
(Marrubium vulgare)

Animals do not like the bitter taste of horehound or the way its seedcases hook themselves firmly into their fur. But older folks can remember making an extract of the leaves and stalks for flavoring candy. Horehound is used as a cough-drop ingredient because it is soothing to the throat, and the strong-tasting tea made from this weed was formerly used to fight colds. Notice the curious way the flowers, which are white, hug the stalks of the rough leaves.

Lamb's-quarters
(Chenopodium album)

Watch for a plant with a silvery sheen to its leaves, which turn red in autumn. Watch also for leaves that are shaped like the footprint of a goose. This is lamb's-quarters, otherwise known as white goosefoot, pigweed, and fat hen. The flowers are greenish and tightly clustered. Young plants, when they are tender, may be eaten raw in salads or boiled like spinach. Many wintertime birds are saved from starvation by eating the fat little seeds of lamb's-quarters.

Dandelion
(flower stalks
to 6 inches high)

Horehound
(to 3 feet high)

Lamb's-quarters
(to 4 feet high)

Wild Mustard, White Mustard, and Black Mustard
(Brassica arvensis, Brassica albus, and Brassica nigra)

Hippocrates recommended the seeds of mustard plants for medicinal purposes. The ancients felt that placing a few mustard seeds under the tongue would prevent it from becoming paralyzed. White mustard (Brassica albus) and black mustard (Brassica nigra) leaves are widely used in salads. Their seeds, when bruised, are used for flavoring sauces, and they contain an oil that is used in making soap. White mustard seeds are used in making mustard plasters, a time-honored remedy for aching joints and sore muscles. In early summer the golden heads of mustard are a familiar sight along our highways and byways. These weeds can quickly take control of a field, and they are the farmers' deadly foe.

Peppermint, and Spearmint
(Mentha piperita, and Mentha spicata)

These two mints are grown for their oil, which is used as a peppermint or spearmint flavoring. Michigan has fields of cultivated peppermint plants, and both mints are grown on the West Coast. Peppermint has rich-green leaves, while spearmint leaves are pale-green. Both plants have pinkish-lavender flowers. These plants are a common sight in wet pastures, in waste places, and along roadsides. Before the American Revolution, colonists were called upon to drink herb teas as a protest against the British tax on tea. Many of these early settlers drank a mixture of peppermint and yarrow.

Purslane, Pursley, or Pusley
(Portulaca oleracea)

Years ago, the low-growing leaves of purslane were gathered and used as potherbs and salad greens. In China, India, Mexico, and some parts of Europe, purslane was, and still is, grown and sold in the food markets. It is a mild-tasting plant and, when boiled or steamed, requires a fair amount of salt. In a salad, the leaves and reddish stems of purslane need such strong-tasting

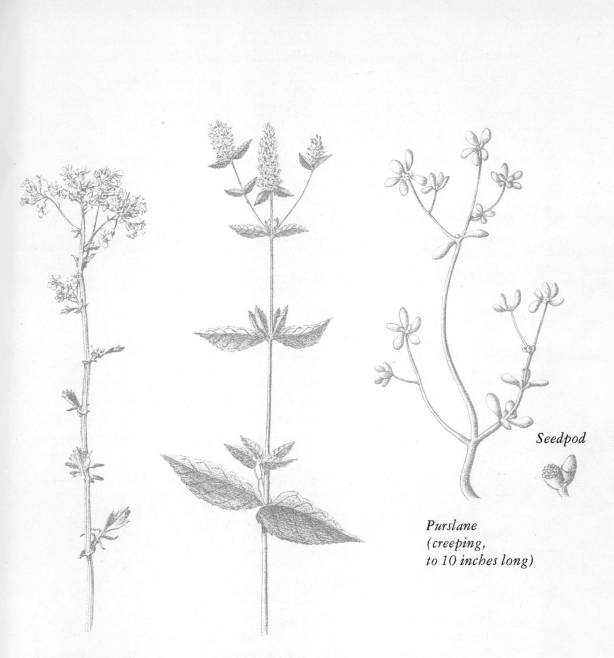

Seedpod

Purslane
(creeping,
to 10 inches long)

Wild mustard
(to 2 feet high)

Peppermint
(to 3 feet high)

41

companions as mustard leaves or lamb's-quarters to make them interesting to eat.

Salsify, Vegetable Oyster, or Oyster Plant
(*Tragopogon porrifolius*)

The fleshy taproots of salsify are edible and taste somewhat like oysters. They are grown in many gardens, particularly in southern Europe. The roots are dug in the late fall or early winter and are stored in cool vegetable cellars in the same way that beets, parsnips, or turnips are. Strangely enough, this plant's myriad purple flowers close by noon.

Winter Cress, or Yellow Rocket
(*Barbarea vulgaris*)

Also known as St. Barbara's cress because its leaves are at their eating best on St. Barbara's Day in early December, this weed survives northern winters. It is seen mostly in fields and meadows and is a member of the Mustard Family. The young stems and leaves, boiled for eating, are quite bitter, therefore many people boil them several times, pouring off the water each time and starting afresh. This method makes the greens less bitter. The tiny flowers are a dazzling yellow and, like those of many other mustard plants, appear in June.

For other edible weeds, see chickweed (page 8), curly dock (page 10), yellow nut grass (page 14), common mallow (page 30), sheep sorrel (page 34), shepherd's purse (page 34), sow thistle (page 34), and pokeweed (page 48).

Salsify
(to 3 feet high)

Wintercress
(to 2 feet high)

43

POISONOUS WEEDS

Bouncing Bet, or Soapwort
(Saponaria officinalis)

The easiest way to identify this weed is to stir some of its crushed leaves in water. If they make soapsuds, you will know you have bouncing Bet. The foam substance in the juice of the leaves, saponin, is poisonous to some people. The pink or white flowers look like heraldic trumpets with 5 petals at one end. Sometimes the petals are doubled in number. Notice that the leaves are attached directly to the stems and have no stalks. You'll find bouncing Bet near abandoned farms, along roadsides, and in neglected fields. It flowers from July to September.

Black Nightshade, and Horse Nettle
(Solanum nigrum, and Solanum carolinense)

The Nightshade Family is a huge one, including some very useful plants, others that are highly poisonous. Among them are potatoes, tomatoes, and eggplants. Black nightshade (Solanum nigrum) is a weed of waste places, particularly of dank, shady spots. Its white flowers nod on bending leafstalks and develop into smooth black berries. Horse nettle (Solanum carolinense) has little tomato-shaped yellow berries, and stiff yellow thorns on its stems. Its flowers are white or pale violet; its leaves and berries are very poisonous. Horse nettle roots plunge deep into the earth and spread around with fiendish determination.

Horsetail
(Equisetum arvense)

When mixed with hay, this weed causes a sickness among horses and cattle known as equisetosis. Horsetail is an odd plant, producing fertile shoots which bear a cone of spores in the early spring. When they die, sterile stems with 8 to 12 branches in whorls appear. They remain until autumn. These

44

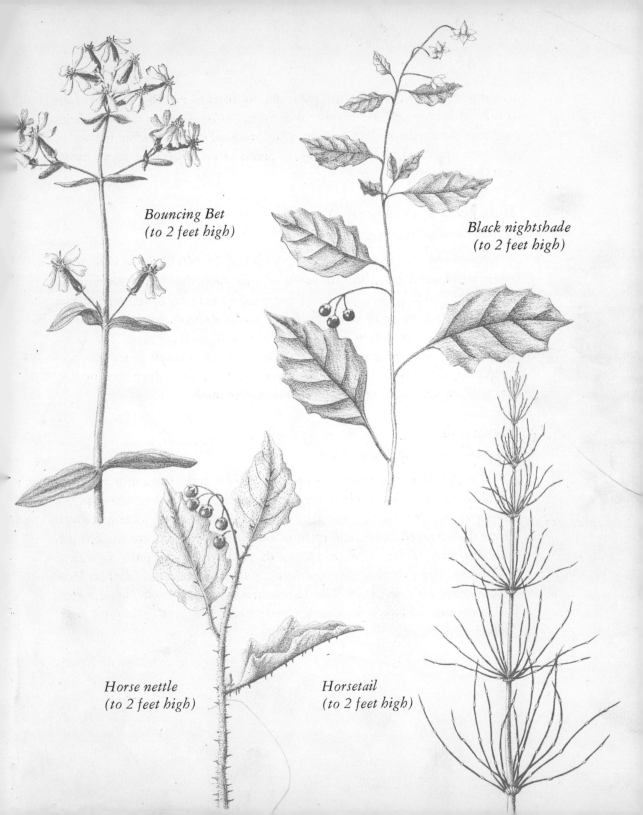

Bouncing Bet
(to 2 feet high)

Black nightshade
(to 2 feet high)

Horse nettle
(to 2 feet high)

Horsetail
(to 2 feet high)

two different growths make the plant doubly hard to identify. Farmers hate this weed because its vicious tuber root system is hard to get rid of in fields and meadows. About 280 million years ago, when the Carboniferous or Coalmaking Period of our earth began, plants of a similar type grew, except that they were much larger.

Jimsonweed, or Thorn Apple
(Datura stramonium)

Jimsonweed settled in Jamestown, Virginia, in 1607, along with some other well-known colonists. Its name, at one time, was Jamestown weed. This plant is deadly poisonous and has a never-to-be-forgotten smell. You can recognize it easily by its odor and by its lovely trumpet-shaped flowers, which are white or purple and appear from July to September. The large, prickly burs protect many flat black seeds, of which a single plant produces thousands. Jimsonweed is one of the sources of atropine, a drug used by doctors to dilate the pupils of the eyes before examination.

Locoweeds
(Astragalus and Oxytropis)

In the West and Southwest where the climate is arid or semiarid, the most troublesome weeds to ranchers are the locoweeds. Several of these plants belong to the Pea Family and they cause a disease called locoism, which effects the nerves of horses, and often of cattle and sheep. *Loco* is the Spanish word for crazy. Three common locoweeds are purple locoweed (*Astragalus mollissimus*), gray or blue locoweed (*Astragalus diphysus*) and Lambert locoweed (*Oxytropis lambertii*). The last-mentioned plant usually has purple, but sometimes white, flowers, resembling sweet peas and blooming from June to September.

Jimsonweed
(to 5 feet high)

Locoweed
(to 20 inches high)

Poison Hemlock
(Conium maculatum)

Into the bubbling caldrons of our finest witches go the roots of the hemlock. The Athenians used a highly poisonous hemlock brew for executing people they considered criminals. Socrates, the great philosopher, died from drinking a cup of hemlock. The weed has been grown in this country as a drug plant. Bordering fields, in meadows, and along roadsides, poison hemlock's feathery foliage reminds one of parsley. One way of identifying this plant is by its long white taproot. Another way is by the purple blotches on its stems. Its shy white flowers are arranged umbrellalike at the tops of the stems.

Poison Ivy, and Poison Oak
(Rhus toxicodendron, Rhus radicans, Rhus diversiloba, Rhus quercifolia)

Everyone should know what these mean plants look like. Poison ivy and its Pacific Coast relative, poison oak, cause an itchy, stingy rash that may spread all over the body. The trouble in identifying the plant is that there are a number of forms and leaf shapes, depending on the area where it is found. The 3 leaflets may be deeply lobed or not; some leaves are thicker than others; some are glossy and some are dull in color. It is best, therefore, to know exactly what the plant looks like in the area where you live, and then to stay far away from it. The flowers have 5 yellow-green petals and are seen in June and July. The fruit is small and cream-colored.

Pokeweed, Poke, or Pigeonberry
(Phytolacca americana)

Sky-high climbs the pokeweed. Sometimes reaching 9 feet, this huge plant is a Dr. Jekyll and Mr. Hyde. Its fleshy roots and its berries are highly poisonous to eat, but its young, leafy sprouts can sometimes be found for sale as greens in the markets of East Coast cities. They, too, may be somewhat

Poison ivy
(climbing,
to 12 feet long)

Poison hemlock
(to 6 feet high)

Pokeweed
(to 9 feet high)

49

poisonous unless they are properly cooked. The Algonquin Indians called the plant "pocan," and used its berries as a dye to color their bodies and clothes. Children use the berry juice, which is quite black, for ink. Never eat pokeberries!

Ragweed
(*Ambrosia artemisiifolia*)

When ragweed pollen fills the autumn air, hay-fever victims fill the air with sneezes. Ragweed stems are rough and hairy, the leaves are lacy and deeply notched. The flower spikes are greenish-white, and a single flower looks like an upside-down turban. A wise farmer plows up ragweed before the flowers appear. In so doing, however, he destroys one of the main winter food sources of quails and grouse — the ragweed seeds.

Common Smartweed, and Lady's Thumb
(*Polygonum hydropiper, and Polygonum persicaria*)

Hydropiper means "water pepper" — a good name for the common smartweed. It loves moisture, and has a fiery leaf juice that causes a burning, stinging sensation on contact with the eyes or skin. Smartweed's close relative is the nonpoisonous lady's thumb, or spotted smartweed. According to legend, when the holes were dug for the three crosses on Calvary, all the uprooted flowers died except the spotted smartweed. It grew sadly on, bearing on each leaf a mark resembling a drop of blood, or a tiny heart.

Sneezeweed
(*Helenium autumnale*)

Milk from cows that have eaten sneezeweed is tainted. The weed is poisonous to many other farm animals. It is common in low, wet pasturelands, and along streams and swamps. The golden-yellow ray flowers are three-toothed and droop downward; the disk flowers are greenish-yellow. The plant blooms from August through October. Strangely, when animals eat the

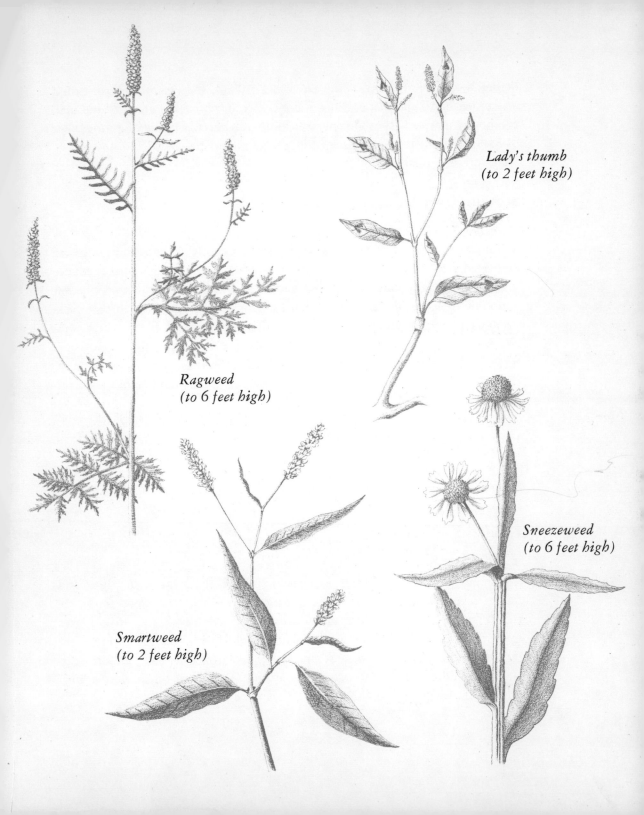

Ragweed
(to 6 feet high)

Lady's thumb
(to 2 feet high)

Sneezeweed
(to 6 feet high)

Smartweed
(to 2 feet high)

flower heads, which have a fine powder on them, they seem to want more and more. But if they eat too many, they often have trouble in breathing and eventually may even die. This plant is known as sneezeweed because the odor of its leaves sometimes causes sneezing; when dried and powdered, the leaves were formerly used as snuff.

Stinging Nettle
(Urtica dioica)

This weed has stinging hairs on its stems. Along the roadsides and in neglected yards you will recognize it by its heart-shaped leaves and its small, greenish flowers blooming on spikes in midsummer. The Scottish people use young nettle leaves like spinach — but they must wear gloves when they pick them. The ancient Egyptians cultivated this plant for its fiber, which was processed and woven into strong fabrics used for making clothing and shelters. Early Americans brewed and drank a tea of nettles, supposedly good in curing rheumatism. Some kinds of Asian nettles are claimed to be powerful enough to kill people with their sting.

For other poisonous weeds, see brake fern (page 18), mayweed (page 30), tansy (page 56), and star-of-Bethlehem (page 62).

WEEDS USED IN MEDICINES

Catnip
(Nepeta cataria)

In years past, catnip tea was used to bring down the fever of smallpox and scarlet fever patients. It makes one perspire, and is therefore good for colds, too. The tea is brewed from either fresh or dried leaves. Catnip is better known for its madcap effect on cats, who delight in sniffing and eating it. In fact, the botanical name means "the cat plant from Nepete," an Etruscan city of early Italy. The flowers, small and in a spike, are whitish, dotted with purple. Catnip belongs to the Mint Family.

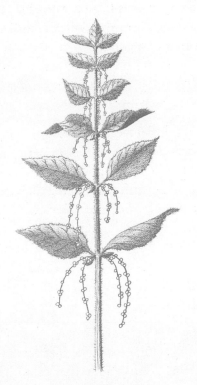

Stinging nettle
(to 3 feet high)

Catnip
(to 3 feet high)

Coltsfoot, or Coughwort
(Tussilago farfara)

Looking somewhat like dandelion heads, the flowers of coltsfoot appear in spring, as early as March. Leaflike scales are pressed tightly to the flower stems. Later on, after the flowering, the true leaves appear. On the undersides of these leaves are long, woolly hairs which are used in some medicines as an emetic. *Tussilago,* the Latin name, comes from a word for "cough" and indicates the plant's reputation as a cough remedy. Coltsfoot's large, rounded leaves are thought to resemble the foot of a colt.

Foxglove
(Digitalis purpurea)

When not in bloom, the handsome foxglove resembles mullein. Its leaves are wrinkled and downy on the undersides. This European native is grown in flower gardens, but in some localities it often pushes and elbows modest garden flowers out of the way. The beautiful, drooping flowers are bell-shaped and flare out into 2 lips at the top. Foxglove flowers of this species are about 2 inches long and are purple or white, depending on the variety. The leaves are the source of one of our most important heart remedies, the drug digitalis.

Indian Hemp, or Choctaw Root
(Apocynum cannabinum)

The root of Indian hemp supplies us with a medicine that acts as an emetic and a cathartic. The plant also contains a milky juice that could be used as a source of rubber. The stem is tough and woody like the bark of a tree. It was used by some Indians for making a coarse fiber. The small, greenish-white, flowers bloom from June to August.

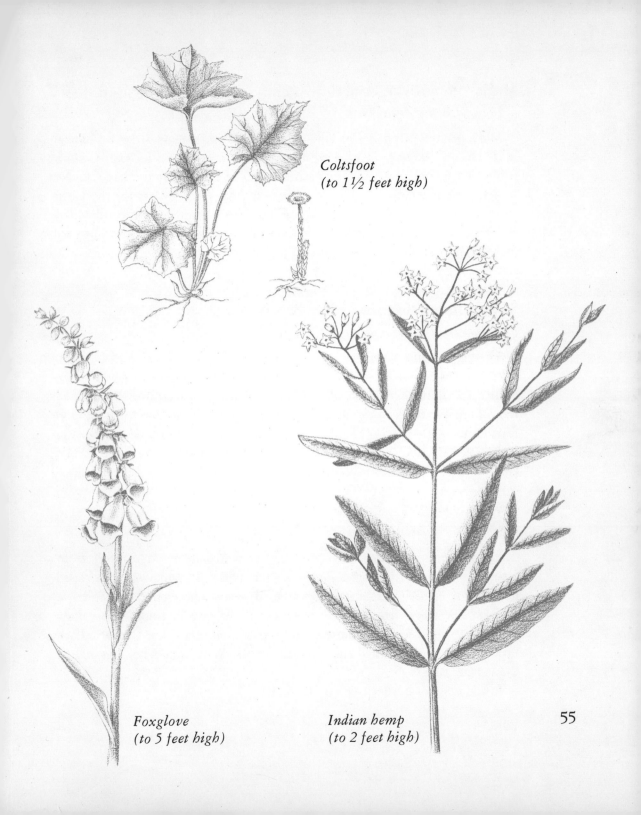

Coltsfoot
(to 1½ feet high)

Foxglove
(to 5 feet high)

Indian hemp
(to 2 feet high)

55

Mock Pennyroyal, American Pennyroyal, or Squawmint
(Hedeoma pulegioides)

Mock pennyroyal makes its home in dry fields and on sun-drenched banks. It is a strong little plant, growing in poor soil to about 18 inches. Its slim, pale-green leaves grow opposite each other. The flowers, at the bases of the leaves, are pinkish-purple. The sweet-smelling foliage accounts for the Latin name, *Hedeoma,* from the Greek meaning "sweet-scented." An oil distilled from the leaves and small stems is used in some medicines and soaps, but more often it is used as a mosquito repellent. Because of this, pennyroyal is sometimes known as mosquito plant.

Tansy, Bitter Buttons, or Golden Buttons
(Tanacetum vulgare)

The tight, yellow buttons of tansy are a familiar sight along our roadsides. Its flowers and leaves were once used by Europeans in several home remedies, and the leaves were also put into puddings for flavoring. Brought by the colonists to this country as a medicinal herb, tansy escaped from the gardens to become a weed. The oil from its stems and leaves contains the chemical tanacetin which, taken in large amounts, is poisonous to humans and animals. Tansy is used in some insecticides because it is a good flea-killer.

Wormwood
(Artemisia absinthium)

In years past, oil from the wormwood was used in medicines and as an insect repellent also. A native European, this graceful plant was often raised in the herb garden. Its bitter oil was used as an ingredient in absinthe, a liqueur. The leaves are 2- or 3-parted and silver-gray in color. The yellow flowers are in loose, open clusters, and blossom from July to October. Each little flower is no more than 1/6-inch across. Wormwood belongs to the Composite Family.

In addition, see burdock (page 20).

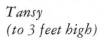

Tansy
(to 3 feet high)

Mock pennyroyal
(to 1½ feet high)

Wormwood
(to 4 feet high)

57

STRANGE AND UNUSUAL WEEDS

Beggar-ticks, or Sticktight
(*Bidens frondosa*)

Beggar-ticks are hitchhikers. From August to December the tough, 2-pronged fruits attach themselves to our clothing when we brush by them in meadows and fields. Animals get them so firmly attached to their fur that in attempting to get rid of them they drive the barbs even deeper and irritate their skin. The more free rides we give these seeds, the more dancing, golden flowers will appear in our meadows next July. Beggar-ticks is a tall plant, to 4 feet in height, with lance-shaped leaves. It loves moist places.

Cocklebur
(*Xanthium orientale*)

The cocklebur is another footloose weed. After country children romp through a patch of it, their clothes are covered with burry passengers, and their dogs dance a merry-go-round, trying to chew the burs out of their tails. Each prickly bur has two seeds, one of which may germinate the first year, while the other waits until the second year. This strange habit explains why cockleburs are hard to defeat: a farmer may destroy one year's growth, only to find a brand-new crop the next year. Young cocklebur plants are poisonous to animals. Cocklebur leaves are large, somewhat heart-shaped, and rough to the touch.

Milkweed
(*Asclepias syriaca*)

A favorite of flies, bees, and butterflies, especially the lovely monarch butterfly, milkweed's fragrant flowers are unusual. When an insect crawls over the blossom in search of nectar, he may find his leg caught in a tiny slit. After a struggle, he gets it free, but now there are waxy pollen grains attached to his leg. In visiting another flower, he leaves the pollen on the

58

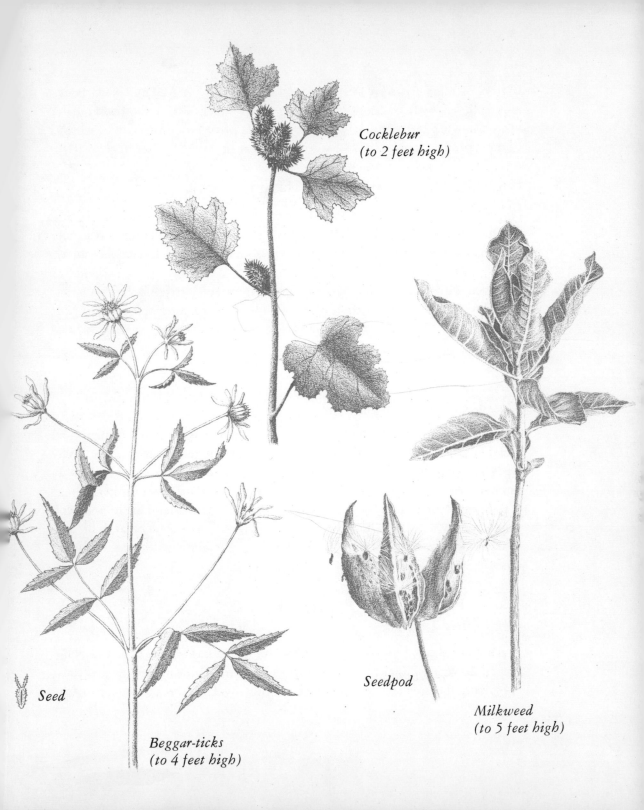

Cocklebur
(to 2 feet high)

Seed

Beggar-ticks
(to 4 feet high)

Seedpod

Milkweed
(to 5 feet high)

stigma, or female part, of the blossom. In time, the familiar milkweed pods appear, filled with seeds, each topped by tufty hairs. When the pods break open, the wind carries the seeds for miles. This plant has a milky juice which country people claim will make warts disappear, if dabbed on them regularly.

Night-flowering Catchfly, or Clammy Cockle
(Silene noctiflora)

This strange plant has fragrant white or pinkish flowers that open at even-tide and close early the following morning. Night moths pollinate the catch-fly. Its stem and leaves are covered with sticky, clammy hairs, and many insects find themselves unhappily and forevermore stuck to them. It is thought that this stickiness prevents crawling insects from robbing the plant of its pollen supply. The leaves near the top of the catchfly have no stalk, while the long narrow base leaves are stemmed.

Russian Thistle
(Salsola kali)

Capable of producing thousands of seeds, each Russian thistle plant is a loose, bushy ball of red stems, sometimes growing 3 feet long. When its seeds are ripe, the thistle breaks off just above the ground and becomes a tumbleweed. It is thought that the plant first came from Russia in the 1870's with a cargo of flaxseed. In the desert country, the Russian thistle is green in summer when many of the other desert plants are brown because of the heat and lack of water. Tough and durable, Russian thistles live through many a severe drought.

Scarlet Pimpernel, or Pimpernel
(Anagallis arvensis)

Also called poor man's weatherglass, this plant has scarlet or white bell-shaped flowers that quickly close up when a storm is brewing. A low, spread-ing plant, the scarlet pimpernel has smooth, oval leaves, opposite to each

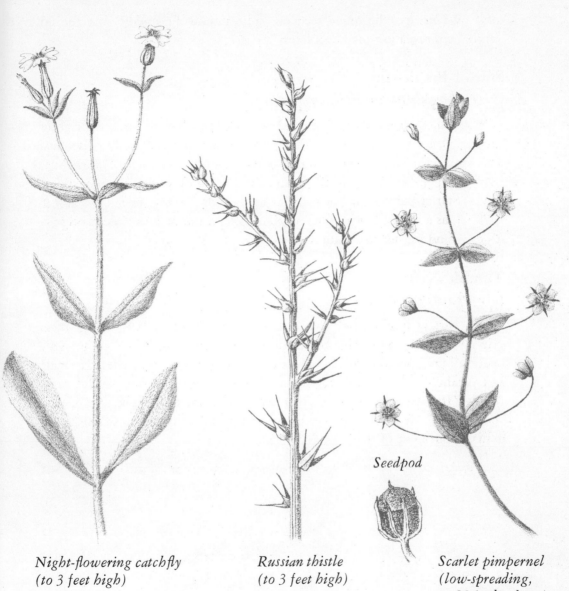

Night-flowering catchfly
(to 3 feet high)

Russian thistle
(to 3 feet high)

Seedpod

Scarlet pimpernel
(low-spreading,
to 20 inches long)

61

other. When ripe, the round seedpods split around the middle, and the lid springs up, revealing myriads of tiny seeds.

Star-of-Bethlehem
(*Ornithogalum umbellatum*)

Also called sleepy dick, this weed opens only when the sun is brightly shining. It is a perennial, reproducing from bulbs, and is entirely poisonous. The long, thin leaves have a lighter-green midrib, and each of the white, star-shaped flowers is enclosed in an envelope of tiny, green-veined floral leaves. Star-of-Bethlehem is a member of the Lily Family. In many states it is grown as a flower, but in some others, people think of it as a weed because it grows and spreads so rapidly.

Tumbleweed
(*Amaranthus albus*)

The curious tumbleweeds, when dried out, curl into a ball, loosen their grip on the soil, and tumble before the wind, spilling seeds as they go. This one is a prairie weed, at home on the dry western plains. Its leaves are small and paddle-shaped. Its flowers, in small green clusters, bloom in July and August. Its stems are whitish. *Amaranthus* is from the Greek, and means "not fading." Many members of the Amaranthus Family are grown in flower gardens, but most of them are too weedy.

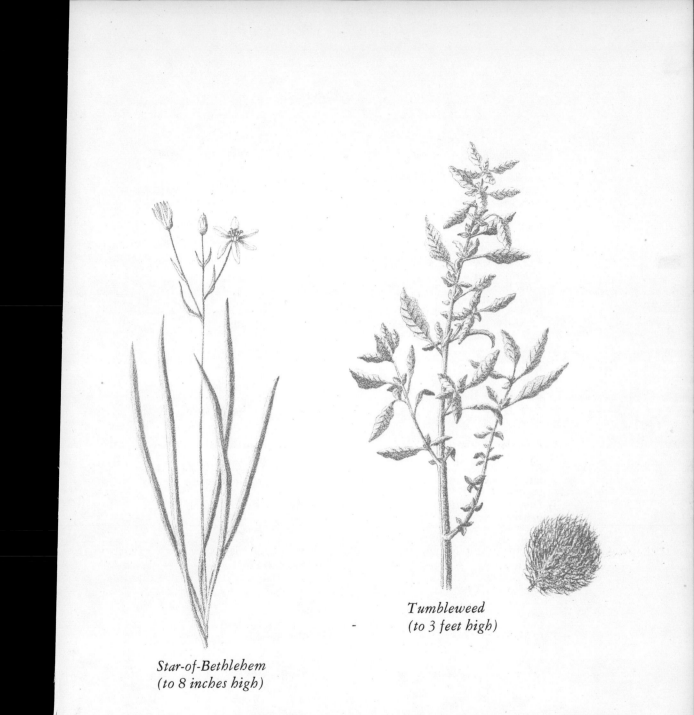

*Tumbleweed
(to 3 feet high)*

*Star-of-Bethlehem
(to 8 inches high)*

63

INDEX